MW00953816

Couponin
How to Start Couponing & Save Money on Groceries

Table of Contents

Chapter 1: How to Start Couponing for Beginners

You may be wondering, how do I start couponing? Well, first you'll need coupons. Coupons are everywhere if you know where to look. In this post, we'll be discussing the best couponing tips for saving money and places to locate those valuable vouchers for groceries.

First let's cover the most common source, the Sunday Newspaper. Every issue of your local Sunday Newspaper regardless of where you live will have a handful of coupon inserts neatly tucked away in the center of the paper. These inserts depending on the sales cycles will feature deals and discounts from Redplum coupons, Smart Source, or P&G Smart Saver.

You can subscribe to receive your local newspaper weekly or you can purchase it directly at most supermarkets or nearby grocery store, newsstands, or gas stations.

Getting Started

To really make the most of your couponing efforts it's couponing 101 to have at least two newspapers worth of inserts at your disposal. Some people prefer to follow the rule of thumb of having one newspaper per household family member but that's only necessary if you're planning on stockpiling which we'll talk more about in a future post.

For general savings on your monthly grocery shopping, two papers will be enough.

Although accumulating coupons is one of the most important steps in this process, try not to get too caught up in the pursuit of coupons.

If your budget is tight and one newspaper is all you can get right now that's okay. There are plenty of coupon sources available and you have time to do more down the road if you choose to.

"Remember the goal is to save money and stress less, not the other way around."

In-store coupons are available directly through certain chains like Target and other major retailers. You can usually print them directly from their websites online.

- **NOTE: You can find a list with all of the links to the websites and resources mentioned in this book on the 'Go-to Resources page.'**

Sometimes if you subscribe to their mailing list they'll send you free in-store coupons via mail as well. A quick search online with the name of your desired grocery store will usually yield good results.

Walmart is one of the most sought after in-store vouchers. There are two places to find Walmart coupons. The first is in their website's printable coupon section and the other is inside the All You Magazine available via subscription or purchase at the retailer.

The All You Magazine is loaded with every current coupon for groceries. If you shop their often you should definitely grab an issue. What's great about All You Magazine is many of the deals have lengthy expiration dates.

Some stores allow shoppers to 'stack' which is the method of using a manufacturer coupon with a store coupon on the same product for a bigger discount. So having a batch of in-stores also is essential.

Many of the manufacturer coupons found in the newspaper inserts can be printed online off of coupon sites like Coupons.com, CouponMom, Smartsource, Redplum, and P&G Everyday.

Looking up specific brands and calling the manufacturer directly to comment on the product can result in receiving free coupons too.

Some more extreme couponers go to coupon clipping service sites like the CouponClippers or Klip2Save offer precut coupons. Ebay also has vendors selling vouchers.

It's always best when you're first learning how to start couponing as a beginner to find and cut the coupons yourself if possible. It's easy to get scammed with bogus or expired coupons when using clipping services, so always be cautious.

Chapter 2: Finding Sales & Deals for Grocery Shopping

In couponing it's the act of buying specific items already on sale and combining them with a coupon that actually saves consumers money. Finding sales and deals for grocery shopping isn't as easy as you may think. Just whipping out a coupon to save 50 cents off a $4.99 product will not equal big savings.

It's finding that $4.99 item on sale for $2.99 and having a $1.00 off coupon and an in-store coupon that you can 'stack' with it giving you an extra $1.50 off of the same product, so you end up only paying 49 cents for $5 item that makes the difference.

Sometimes the process of stacking coupons along with Bogo deals will result in getting the item for free which is one of the ways to save money and answers the question of 'how does extreme couponing work?' much like the coupon television shows, it's possible to accumulate massive stock piles of products.

"If you don't know about it, you can't clip it."

Every couponer should have multiple 'Go-to Sources' for finding the best coupons, sales, and deals for grocery savings. I will routinely recommend sites that I personally use or consider as quality sources that you can bookmark on your computer and refer to when you're working on your grocery lists. You can never have enough resources.

 Most locations have an estimated sales cycle length average of six weeks. Prices will vary during the period from full price all the way down to its lowest mark down. This is where the second step in couponing comes into play, timing and deal finding. Southern Savers has a free handy Weekly Store Ad Schedules and Buy Price List that you can download to help keep track of when certain items hit their peak.

They also have tons and tons of information on how to start couponing that every beginner should read. The site is not only on my list of 'Go-to Sources' but it's also part of our list of top coupon database websites.

Coupon database websites and or blogs are the best places to find sales and deals to match up with your coupons. These information hubs lists all the product items for each supermarket chain or drugstore that have currently went on sale.

Couponers can view the item name; its original price and the reduced sale price along with any special buy 1 get 1 free deal that might be associated with the purchase of that item. All databases are updated every Thursday and Sunday.

'Go-to Sources' for Coupon Databases and Finding Sales & Deals for Groceries

Another way to find out about the latest sales is through forums and social media sites like Instagram. Coupon forums and message boards have special deal sections where members can post bargains they've found in their area.

It's a great strategy to get items that are not listed in the database but are available for the select few who are in-the-know.

For those savvy shoppers that are into social networking the photo sharing app and site Instagram has a surprising amount of couponers on-board taking snapshots of their recent deals and stockpiles. Simply enter into the search tab #clearance or #coupon to see photos of items just purchased on sale.

Facebook couponing groups also provide good sources from time to time as well. Try to join one based near your location for better results. Below is a list of 'Go-to Sources' message boards that you can check out. Be sure to brush up on your coupon lingo to make corresponding on the boards easier. Most members are veterans and often use abbreviations when listing deals.

- Hot Coupon World
- A Full Cup
- We Use Coupons
- Coupon Forum
- Slick Deals
- Deal Catcher
- Fat Wallet
- Gotta Deal
- Big Big Forums
- My Coupons

Chapter 3: Essential Tools & Tips for Saving Money

Welcome to the world of couponing. Things can get cluttered quick so it's vital to be armed with the necessary tools and organization system to make things run smoothly. We'll go more into depth on the coupon supplies you need to get started and how to use them in the next chapter 'How to Organize Your Coupons' but for now, I want to give you a quick rundown of the things you'll need.

Essential Couponing Supplies

- Scissors
- Hard 3 Ring Binder or Zipped Binder/ Trapper Keeper Style (it's up to you, matter of preference)
- Baseball Card or Photo Page Protectors
- Tab Dividers for Binder
- File Box (if you'll using the file box storing system instead of binders)
- Hanging Folders (file box system)
- Calculator (small pocket or you can use your smartphone)
- Writing utensil / Marker (pen, pencil, or highlighter, again matter of preference)

And that's it; you're now ready to conquer those rollback prices!

Most of these couponing supplies you probably already have laying around your house. I recommend only buying the items you need in order to save money. Many of us already have a pair of scissors, pens, pencils, calculator, an old file box or no longer in use binder that can be cleared out, dusted off and repurposed as a coupon book.

Chapter 4: How to Organize Your Coupons

Couponing can quickly become a daunting task if you're not organized. Like most things in life organization is important. When you're starting out it's often overwhelming, so having a good system in place will make the process seem quicker and much easier. Couponing is slighting more complex than just clipping a deal out of the newspaper. There are specific supplies, methods, and calculations that are involved to cut your monthly grocery bill and save the big bucks.

One of the essential tools for couponers that were mentioned in the checklist is a quality binder or file box for storing and organizing your weekly coupons. Although, most pros prefer the binder over the file box it's still a matter of personal preference and completely up to you. Choose whatever you feel most comfortable with. Both methods will work.

 I personally prefer the binder method, because it's more convenient for me to flip through the pages and see everything at once. I like to have all of my coupons pre-clipped and ready for when that particular item goes on sale. File boxes are great for those individuals that want to store flyers without having them visible and like to clip right before they go to the store.

How to Organize Your Coupons with Coupon Binder and File Box Methods

Remember, developing an organized system is the core goal. Don't focus so much on the cosmetics. There are a lot of websites out there that sell and promote fancy designer coupon organizers and colorful inserts but they cost $40 and up. If you want to splurge, I won't stop you but the whole point of couponing is to save money. Why blow unnecessary dollars for supplies? Aim more for durability to meet your organizational needs. A three ring binder from Office Depot or Staples costs roughly $2.78 to $9. A plastic file box is around $10 to $15 give or take.

You'll also need photo pages and dividers which can be purchased for cheap if you don't already have them. If you're like me and happen to scrapbook or have a bunch of photo albums with extra page inserts in the back, you can use those for now and save yourself a little extra cash and time by not having to run immediately to the store to purchase new packs of pages.

If you do need to buy them they can be purchased at the same office supply outlets in packs of 10 for around $3.59 to $5. Some ladies prefer to use Trading Card pages while others lean more towards the 4x6 multi direction photo pages for storing coupons. Either or will work.

I like to use a combination of the two along with full photo pages to keep catalinas or whole page ads that I might want to review and clip out at a later date. It's up to you. If you're using the file box method you'll need a set of 20 hanging folders, instead of photo pages.

Dividers are slightly more expensive then photo pages starting out at $4.50 and often as high as $7. I know what you're thinking ….. $7 bucks that's highway robbery, lol!

Do I really need them? Unfortunately, the answer is yes. Dividers play an important role in the organization of your coupons. It's impossible to know what category of items you're looking at and to be able to quickly go from frozen foods to pantry or canned goods without them.

Step-by-Step Guide for Making Your Own Coupon Binder Dividers and Saving Tons of Money

But lucky for you, you've found this site and I'm going to give you a quick money saving tip to avoid paying for overpriced dividers if your local office supply store doesn't have a decent deal on them.

Simply make your own. Most people have extra manila folders stuffed in a desk or file box somewhere that's not being used or is no longer needed.

STEP 1:

Grab a pair of scissors, a paper hole puncher, and pen or whatever other items you'd like to use to write the label with along with some file folders new or used and binder that you have laying around.

STEP 2:

Cut the folder in half, following straight down the fold line and use the side with the visible tab as your first divider. Open up your binder and line the folder alongside the rings.

Using a pencil (I prefer the pencil just in case my measurement is somewhat off and I need to erase it but a pen will work also) make a small mark estimating the best place to punch the necessary holes.

Take a quick glance to make sure it will properly fit inside and punch away.

STEP 3:

Repeat with another folder until you have one for every category you plan on using in your binder.

STEP 4:

When you're ready simply take an already made label or marker or pen and write down the appropriate category on each tab.

If you're working with used folders with tabs that have been previously written on, you can cover up the tab with Scotch Masking Tape and write over the tape. If you don't have any tape handy you can glue a piece of plain copy paper trimmed to fit the tab on top of the old label and then write over that as well.

Now you have your own coupon binder that you made yourself.

A lot of people get side-tracked with the stigma of being a couponer and having this fancy binder. If you want a fancy binder and don't mind spending the extra couple bucks to get one by all means knock yourself out.

No one else will be flipping through the pages but you. It can be a 'plain Jane or upscale Elaine'. It doesn't really matter; it's your personal binder. It just needs to be functional.

Whether you organize your coupons using a coupon binder or the file box method it's all about being able to easily access your coupons when you need them.

Chapter 5: Couponing Tips & Tricks

When it comes to couponing the more tips and tricks and effective strategies you know, the higher your savings, and that's what it's all about. Below are some great little known tips to help beginners and even veteran savvy shoppers get the most out of their coupons.

Tip #1 – Buy on Sale

Always wait for your coupon item to be on sale before you buy it. Remember, it's the purchase of an item already on sale and stacking that coupon with it that really saves you money.

Tip #2 – Stack Whenever Possible

Stack coupons whenever possible, the act of using a manufacturer coupon with a store coupon on the same product will give you the best deal. Although you can't use two manufacturer coupons on the same item you can always stack a manufacturer coupon with a store coupon.

Tip #3 – Only Toss When Expired

Don't toss out your coupons too early. Keep your coupons till the expiration date because you never know when a store will have that particular product on sale.

Tip #4 – Look for Tag Coupon Items

When grocery shopping always look for items with hanging tag coupons on them, coupons with overages, and coupons with X amount off of any product.

Tip #5 – Search for BOGO Deals

A helpful BOGO stockpiling trick to use when you catch an item on sale listed as Buy 1 Get 1 Free, if you can find a coupon for that same item with Buy 1 Get 1 Free you can use it with the sale item to get both products for nothing.

Another method that shoppers can do when they find a product on sale priced as BOGO, is to find two coupons for that same product and use both coupons for the purchase, one for the one product and one on the second item which when combined with the sale will allow you to snag the items for free or at an extremely low price depending on the amount discounted from the coupon used.

Tip # 6 – Read Your Coupons

Remember to pay attention to your coupon details. Take the time to read them fully, the product pictures can be misleading, always follow the fine print. You don't want to get to the register and in the middle of checkout find out your product doesn't match the coupon.

Tip #7 – Remember the Two Sunday Newspapers Minimum

To get coupons try to buy or subscribe in order to receive at least two Sunday Newspapers.

Tip #8 – Snag Free Coupons with Samples

Take advantage of the sample stand in grocery stores they usually have free coupons available that you can grab along with the sample.

Tip #9 – Use Peelie Stickers

While shopping stay on the lookout for peelie stickers on products. They are coupons, despite their appearance and can help.

Tip #10 – Print Coupons Up to Limit

For printable coupons, there is a limit of two prints per computer. You can print more if you have multiple computers in your home and hook the printer up to each individual computer to print.

And for individuals that don't own multiple computers you can print coupons out at your local library via their printer but it does cost 10 cents a page.

Tip #11 – Go Small with Low Value Coupons

When you have low value coupons like 50 cents off ect opt to buy the smaller package or version of the item to get the best deal. If the coupon does not exclude trial size, you can get an even lower priced to free product.

Tip #12 – Ask about Discounts

Ask your local stores when they have Military Discount Days and take advantage of them if you're a military veteran or family member.

Tip #13 – Use Store Cards

When you coupon at CVS use your CVS Extra Care Card to receive extra care bucks with every purchase. Also remember to stop at their Coupon Center booth located inside the store and scan your extra care card for free printable coupons.

You can scan your card twice per day at the machine for coupons. It's a great way to stock up.

Tip #14 – Check out Southern Savers

For finding deals on specific items visit Southern Savers. They have an awesome item search feature for finding sales on a particular product or brand that you prefer or happen to have a coupon for. It's an excellent deal research tool to use.

For Wal-Mart deals and coupon sites like iheartthemart.com and ladysavings.com often have helpful printable sales lists available. Take advantage of these easily accessible printable resources online.

Tip #15 – Follow Sale Cycles

If you're stockpiling always rely on sales cycles and stock for 6 weeks on certain items, and things you have to have only get enough for 1 week.

Chapter 6: How to Save Big Bucks on Cosmetics

For savvy shoppers that are also fellow cosmetic junkies, saving big on makeup and beauty items is a must. Although it may seem like mission impossible to reduce the costs of high priced name brand items like Revlon, Maybelline and Cover Girl, it is attainable.

If you know where to look with a little initiative you can save tons on your cosmetics.

Beauty coupons can be found in magazines, newspaper inserts, and online. Walgreens, Target, and Wal-Mart are excellent places to find and use coupons to buy various beauty items such as makeup, lotion, bath and hair care products.

All You Magazine has a mix of food and personal care item vouchers inside. Target's cartwheel option also features sales of that nature.

If your local Bed Bath & Beyond has a cosmetic section in it you can use the '20% off purchase coupon' that comes in advertisement flyer mailers to save at checkout. It applies to all items sold in the store, how awesome is that?!

Remember to always shop with the current sales in mind, on the Ulta website they usually have deals posted and online coupon codes that can be entered at checkout for a reduced price.

Mix and match bath and hair care items, buy 2 get 2 free deals and free 14 piece gift set with a purchase of any $19.50 of select ULTA brand products are great offers to take advantage of to help stock up on cosmetics.

Coupon codes are often overlooked as a money-saver but they are actually gold mines. $3.50 off of any $10 purchase is a great deal especially when you're just in need of one particular item.

At Ulta they feature one new coupon like that each week. It's available as a printable or can be used as an online code at checkout.

Most name brands have a member club that you can join for free. Becoming a member can help you score your cosmetics at a lower price.

For example if you're a fan of Freeman products, you can go to their website and sign up for their newsletter/mailing list. They send daily, weekly, or monthly emails directly to you notifying you of special sales and discounts being offered.

I suggest creating a new email account and using that address to sign up for coupons and various newsletters that way you're have all your deals and sales coming in one inbox and you won't miss or mix it up with personal or work related messages.

Search online for your favorite brands and beauty stores like Sally, Sephora, and Image and in turn for a little personal information they'll keep you up-to-date on all the latest deals and coupons. They usually offer free samples with manufacturer coupons in the mail too. You'd be surprised at all the cool new facial masks, eye cream, and makeup samples you'll get shipped straight to your door. Being frugal definitely doesn't mean you can't be glamorous. No one has to know you got it for free unless you want them to know.

Chapter 7: Rebates 101 – Ibotta VS Checkout 51

Two extremely popular apps that many couponers are buzzing about these days are the Ibotta and the Checkout 51 app. Despite their different features and styles they both allow users to earn and redeem rebates from their weekly shopping excursions.

Rebates in a Nutshell

If you're not familiar with the term rebate it's basically a type of promo sale that manufacturers use to make customers want to risk buying their product.

Mail-in rebates (MIR) work similar to coupons but instead of receiving your discount at checkout, the individual pays the full price and mails back the coupon or receipt for the rebate amount. Then the company sends a check for the set amount described for that particular rebate to you.

Many couponers like rebates because you feel like you're getting a good deal, plus who doesn't like receiving a check in the mail, right.

An instant rebate is when an item is on sale in the store but the reduced price isn't applied until checkout. They are usually marked.

For example a product might be tagged at $7.99 with a side note saying with a $5 instant rebate, which simply means you're only be charged $2.99 at the register.

Mobile apps like Ibotta and Checkout 51 are standard rebates that instead of mailing the receipt back you electronically send it, resulting in receiving your money quicker.

How it works, exactly?

Well, you log into the application through your Smartphone and browse down the list of various offers. Select the ones you want to buy and add those items to your grocery list. Just shop as you normally do but remember to keep the receipt, you'll need it in order to redeem your rebates.

When you get home usually after you've put away of your items or whenever you get time, just remember all receipts and offers have a one week time frame for redemption.

So, if you're sometimes forgetful like I am, it's best to upload your receipt the day of purchase, but not necessary. To upload your receipt and claim your rebate simply tap on the claim tab and your phone's camera will automatically turn on, snap a photo of the entire receipt and tap submit when you're done.

If you have a long receipt like most couponers do, simply take several snapshots tapping the 'add section' to continue capturing the rest of the proof of purchase.

It usually takes 24 hours to process but most of the time it's approved sooner than that.

So, Ibotta OR Checkout 51?

Ibotta's slogan is 'Cash Not Coupons' and Checkout 51's tagline is 'Buy groceries, Get cash back,' much like their motto's both of these rebate sites differ but not by much. If I had to summarize each application in one world or less, Ibotta would be 'flashy' and Checkout 51 would be 'simple.'

Ibotta is very cutting edge and web 2.0-ish. When users search through available rebates they have several options to earn. They can learn a fact, play trivia, take a poll, like on Facebook, or watch a video. There are typically three different options available with each item with tasks being worth anywhere from $0.25 to $1.50 depending on the offer.

Checkout 51 has a really modest dashboard and users do not get extra earning options along with their rebates for posting on Facebook or watching a video like Ibotta does.

Just select your items, buy them, and then upload a snapshot of your receipt. No frills or thrills with this app, it's simple and to the point. The payment option is traditional also.

The cash-out minimum is $20 and they mail you a check like almost as if it was a traditional mail-in rebate.

Ibotta's minimum cash-out amount is $5 and they don't mail checks. Users receive a direct deposit payment to their Paypal or Venmo account or they can choose a gift card in varied amounts for Starbucks, iTunes, or Redbox Movie Rental.

So, what's the best pick? Hmm-mm, that's a tough one.

It all depends on your personality. If you're more old school and not familiar with the Android or iPhone functions and just want a quick way to snag a few extra rebates but not really concerned about immediate payouts then Checkout 51 would be a good fit for you.

If you're into social media networking sites like Facebook, have a PayPal account, and want to get paid quickly than Ibotta is the better choice.

Personally, I have both. It's free to join and you can still use coupons with your purchases, it doesn't affect the rebates.

Using multiple rebate apps and sources is also a good way to double your savings for the same product.

Chapter 8: Coupon Lingo Quick Reference

Couponing can almost feel like learning a new language at times. If you've ever watched the cable television series, "Extreme Couponers," it seems difficult. All the deals and calculations to gain that perfect $0.00 checkout. Not to mention the various lingo and abbreviations used and often printed onto the coupons itself.

One of the first things that downright confused me when I started my adventure in frugal shopping was the 'one coupon per purchase' phrase. I immediately thought, "Huh, how can you save money if you're only allowed one coupon at checkout? What the heck is a Publix and isn't "Bogo a good deal on shoes?" Yes I admit, I thought that … lol.

 If you ever wondered the same, it's okay. As a beginner it's allowed. I was to know that the one coupon term referred to the item not your entire transaction. I live in Ohio and I had no idea that a 'Publix' was a popular supermarket when other couponers mentioned it online, since our major grocery store chains here are Kroger and Meijers. But it's a process.

Everyone starts from somewhere and if I can figure it out, I know you guys can too. Couponing is a skill that we can all learn to help us go beyond simply saving money but lead us to financial freedom. In this world it's always more you can learn.

With that said, let's tackle the infamous jargon spoken by couponers. Below is a list of some of the most common coupon lingo:

AC – after coupon

ALA – As Low As – Best case scenario, depending on which coupon you use and what the sale price is the price will be as low as…

AR – after rebate – the cost of the item after you receive your rebate

ASAV – Any Size, Any Variety

B1G1 – Buy one get one. This stands for buy one get one FREE but sometimes it's followed by other wording such as B1G1 50% off which means buy one get another at the 50% discount

B2G1 – Buy two items get one free.

BOGO – Buy one get one. Another way of writing the B1G1 as stated above

BOLO – Be On the Look Out

Catalina/CAT – refers to a coupon from a machine next to the cash register that dispenses coupons after your cash register receipt prints. These can usually be used like cash on your next purchase. If they say "manufacturer's coupon" you can usually use them at other stores.

Cartwheel – Target Discounts in the form of % off certain items. This can be used via Smartphone app or printing the list and barcode on paper. This can be used at Target stores as a discount in addition to both a manufacturer coupon and a store coupon. The % is calculated on the item price less any Target coupon but before the price is discounted by the manufacturer coupon.

CO or C/O – cents off

DND – Do not double/Does not double – Sometimes found on specific manufacturers coupons.

Doubled/Double coupon – a coupon redeemed for double the face value, depends on store policy. Many stores will double coupons for $0.50 or less giving you a deduction of double that amount.

Exp – Expires/Expiration date

GDA – Good Deal Alert

HT – Hangtag – a tag hanging from an item that includes information and/or a coupon. Also sometimes referred to as a wine tag.

Inserts – Coupons packets found in Sunday newspapers, generally RedPlum and SmartSource but occasionally P&G, GM or others.

In-Ad / IA – Coupons that come in the weekly store ad, most likely found by the entrance of that particular store.

ISO = In Search Of – Chat lingo usually used in comments and message boards regarding something that person is looking for (coupons, deals)

IVC – Instant Value Coupon

Loyalty Card – A card you sign up for at the particular store where you shop, usually offering you additional discount prices/savings.

Matchups – A listing of available coupons that "match" the specific items listed, are usually in a store sales ad, that can further reduce the purchase price.

MF / MFG / MFR – Manufacturer – Usually referring to a coupon offered by the product manufacturer as opposed to a coupon offered by the store

MIR – Mail in Rebate – Offer that requires you to mail a completed form and usually a receipt and UPC proving you purchased a specific item in return for some amount of money back.

MQ – Manufacturer coupon

MRP – Manufacturer's retail price

NSL or NSR – No size limit/restriction

OOP – Out of pocket – The cash you actually pay to the cashier after coupons/discounts

OYNO / OYNP – On your next order / On your next purchase

OVERAGE – Same as "moneymaker". Coupon amount exceeds item price resulting in a reduction against the total of your transaction or cash back in some stores.

Peelie – Coupons found on actual products that you "peel" off to use

PM – Price Match. One store reducing your register price to match the lower price at another store. Can also mean private message if used in chat/forum.

POP – Proof of Purchase – bar code located on product

Printable – Internet printable coupon – print from your computer

PSA – Price starting at – the lowest priced product

RC – Rain Check – signed slip from store allowing an item to be purchased at sale prices in the future when item is no longer on sale. Received from store when the particular sale item is sold out at the time of your visit. Not all stores write RC's

Rebate – An offer by the manufacturer to try a product and then submit the proof (usually the UPC and/or receipt) to get all or some of the purchase price back. These can be MIR's or sometimes submitted online or via email.

RR or RRs – Register Rewards

Stack/stacking – Using a store coupon and a manufacturer coupon on a single item to get an even lower price

Stockpile – The combined items or storage area for large quantities of extra stock. The storage area of items purchased through the process of couponing that are not currently being used.

TMF – Try me free – some products have a mail in rebate that refunds the money you spent on the purchase to get you to try the product

WSL – While supplies last

WYB – When you buy

There's an awesome coupon 'dictionary' of sorts on the website TheCouponingCouple.com that extends and goes further in-detail on common coupon abbreviations and chat room lingo. It's a life-saver. The entire website is definitely bookmark worthy. They also feature daily deals and have lots of other information for beginners.

You're Now Ready to Start Couponing & Saving Money on Groceries

This guide was created to help you get started and alleviate some of the long hours beginners often spent ISO (coupon lingo for 'in search of') answers to the short but complex question: How do I start couponing?

Hopefully these chapters have provided you with a solid base knowledge on the 'how to' process of couponing.

Remember the goal is to save money and stress less. Knowing how to use coupons properly and taking action will result in big savings on your next trip to the grocery store. Use this book as a reference and keep on clipping!

Go-to Resources & Additional Information

Below is a list of all of the websites referenced throughout this guide:

- RedPlum – http://www.redplum.com

- SmartSource – http://www.smartsource.com

- P&G Everyday - https://www.pgeveryday.com

- Target - http://coupons.target.com

- Walmart - http://coupons.walmart.com

- All You Magazine - http://www.allyou.com

- Coupon Mom – http://www.couponmom.com

- CouponClippers – http://thecouponclippers.com

- Klip2Save – http://www.klip2save.com

- Ebay – http://www.ebay.com

- Hot Coupon World - https://www.hotcouponworld.com/community

- A Full Cup - http://www.afullcup.com

- We Use Coupons - http://www.weusecoupons.com

- Coupon Forum - http://www.couponforum.org

- Slick Deals - http://slickdeals.net/forums/forumdisplay.php?f=10

- Deal Catcher - https://www.dealcatcher.com/forums

- Fat Wallet - https://www.fatwallet.com/forums/online-coupon-trading

- Gotta Deal - http://www.gottadeal.com

- Big Big Forums - http://www.bigbigforums.com

- My Coupons - https://www.mycoupons.com

- Southern Savers – http://www.southernsavers.com

- Ulta Beauty – http://www.ulta.com

- Ibotta – http://ibotta.com/register?friend=hhtycw

- Checkout 51 – https://www.checkout51.com

- The Couponing Couple – http://www.thecouponingcouple.com

- How to Start Couponing - http://howtostartcouponing.blogspot.com

CPSIA information can be obtained
at www.ICGtesting.com
Printed in the USA
LVHW032015280320
651507LV00043B/2987